123s With Tonellio

Written by: Tony Lumpkin

Illustrated by: Maya Henderson

T. Lump Book Publishing

Upper Marlboro, MD

Published by:

T. Lump Book Publishing

Email: TLumpPub@gmail.com

Tony Lumpkin, Publisher

Yvonne Rose/Quality Press.info, Book Packager

Illustrator: Maya Henderson

Copyright ©2021 by Tony Lumpkin

ISBN #: 978-1-0879-0435-1

Library of Congress Control Number: 2021916271

This Book Belongs To:

_____

Dedicated To:

Oliver, Mary, Jewell,
Robert and Melvin.

1
ONE

2

TWO

6 six

MATCHING GAME

1

2   5   8

3   6   9

4   7   10

POINT TO THE WORD THAT MATCHES THE NUMBER.

THREE TEN FIVE

SIX ONE

SEVEN EIGHT

FOUR

NINE

TWO

ABOUT THE AUTHOR

 My name is Tony Lumpkin. I grew up in Washington, DC. I am a United States Postal worker of 34 years. I have two kids which are now young adults. I have two grandsons that are 3 years and 1 year old.

What inspired me to write this book is taking my kids to the playground and running around with them and feeding the ducks at the duck pond. Also, coaching their basketball team of ages 4-6. In 2007-2013 I was a track and field coach for Special Olympics. Then for several years playing Santa at the local recreation centers and church.

I believe that kids should have fun while learning because learning should be fun!

This is my first children's book with more to come.

CPSIA information can be obtained
at www.ICGtesting.com
Printed in the USA
JSHW010008290622
27571JS00001B/1